Geography Zone: Landforms™

Exploring
MOUNTAINS

Melody S. Mis

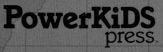
PowerKiDS
press.

New York

To Bill, Christie, Chase and Chris Heavener

Published in 2009 by The Rosen Publishing Group, Inc.
29 East 21st Street, New York, NY 10010

First Edition

Editor: Nicole Pristash
Book Design: Julio Gil
Photo Researcher: Jessica Gerweck

Photo Credits: Cover, pp. 5, 7, 9, 13, 15, 17, 19, 21 Shutterstock.com; p. 11 © Ed Darack/Getty Images.

Library of Congress Cataloging-in-Publication Data

Mis, Melody S.
  Exploring mountains / Melody S. Mis. — 1st ed.
      p. cm. — (Geography zone. Landforms)
  Includes index.
  ISBN 978-1-4358-2715-8 (library binding) — ISBN 978-1-4358-3113-1 (pbk.)
ISBN 978-1-4358-3119-3 (6-pack)
  1. Mountains—Juvenile literature. I. Title.
  GB512.M57 2009
  551.43'2—dc22
                                          2008027557

Manufactured in the United States of America

Contents

What Is a Mountain? 4

Mountain or Hill? 6

Bending Earth 8

Rising Rock 10

Mountains of Fire 12

Dome Mountains 14

Life on Mountains 16

The Rocky Mountains 18

Life in the Rockies 20

People and Mountains 22

Glossary 23

Index 24

Web Sites 24

A mountain is a landform that rises above the land around it. A mountain is tall, and it generally has a **peak**. Mountains are found in many parts of the world. In fact, you may even see a mountain outside your window right now!

There is a lot to learn about mountains. Some mountains stand alone, and others are a part of a group of mountains, called a range. Animal and plant life on mountains is plentiful, too. Let's take a look at different types of mountains and visit one of the best-known mountain ranges in the world.

4

These mountains are part of the Teton Range
in Grand Teton National Park, in Wyoming.

Hills are often mixed up with mountains. This is because mountains and hills look alike. Mountains are taller than hills, though. Mountains are generally more than 2,000 feet (610 m) tall, and their sides can be steep. Mountains are often pointed or **jagged** at the top as well.

A hill, though, is more rounded at the top than a mountain. A hill is not very steep either. Many hills are mountains that **eroded** over a long period of time.

Mountains take a long time to form. This is because most mountains are formed by slow movements inside Earth.

These hills in California have a smooth, rounded shape. Many people call hills like these rolling hills because of their shape.

Earth is made up of several **layers**. The top layer is called the crust. Huge sheets of rock, called plates, make up the crust. When the plates move, they can push against each other, causing the crust to fold. This means that the rocks bend and **wrinkle** on top of the crust. This folding of the crust forms mountains with jagged peaks, called fold mountains.

Fold mountains are the most common type of mountains in the world. Some of the best-known fold mountains are the Himalayas, in Asia, and the Andes, in South America.

This is Mount Everest, in the Himalayas. At 29,029 feet (8,848 m), Everest is the highest mountain in the world.

The Sierra Nevada, in California, is a range of fault-block mountains. Fault-block mountains are made by cracks, or breaks, in the ground. Sometimes, the rocky plates that make up Earth's crust pull **apart**. When this happens, it causes the crust to crack in some places. These cracks are called faults. Faults cause the crust to break up into blocks of rock. Some of the blocks drop down while the other blocks rise up. This forms fault-block mountains.

The sides of fault-block mountains are often different from one another. One side is steep, which makes it hard to climb. The other side has a more rounded **slope**.

This is where the Sierra Nevada meets Owens Valley. A fault caused blocks of rock to rise up, which formed these fault-block mountains.

Have you ever seen a volcano? A volcano is a volcanic mountain. Volcanic mountains are made in a different way from fold or fault-block mountains. Volcanic mountains are formed by **magma** found deep inside Earth.

As magma moves underground, it sometimes breaks through cracks in Earth's crust. Once magma is above ground, it is called lava. As the lava cools, it hardens into rock. Over time, the rock builds up and forms a volcanic mountain.

Many of the world's volcanic mountains are found in the Pacific Ocean. In fact, the world's largest volcanic mountain is Mauna Loa, in Hawaii.

Popocatépetl is a stratovolcano in Mexico. Stratovolcanoes are cone-shaped volcanoes made up of lava and dust that have built up over time.

Dome mountains are formed by magma as well. However, a dome mountain is different because the magma does not break through Earth's crust, as it does in a volcanic mountain. Instead, when magma pushes up under the crust, the magma forces the crust to bend into the shape of a dome, or bump. This bump can grow high enough to become a dome mountain.

You can find a half-dome mountain in California's Yosemite National Park. It is believed that when a large mass of ice, called a glacier, moved through the valley, the other half of the dome mountain broke off!

Half Dome is one of the most common places to visit in Yosemite National Park. People come from all over the world to climb the mountain.

A mountain is home to many living things. At the lowest part of a mountain, animals like foxes, deer, and squirrels live. There are also owls, rabbits, and flies. You can find plants, such as pine trees, bushes, and wildflowers, on mountains as well.

At the top of a mountain, the weather can get very cold and windy. Animals that live on this part of a mountain have thick fur to **protect** them. **Yaks** live in the high peaks of the Himalayas. **Llamas** are found in the Andes. Grizzly bears live in the Rocky Mountains.

This yak is looking for grass to eat on a mountain slope in the Himalayas. Some yaks live on mountain slopes as high as 19,685 feet (6,000 m).

The Rocky Mountains, or Rockies, are some of the best-known mountains in the United States. More than 100 mountain ranges make up the Rockies. They run more than 3,000 miles (4,800 km), from Canada all the way down to New Mexico.

The Rockies' highest mountains are in Colorado. Colorado has about 50 mountains that reach 14,000 feet (4,267 m). The highest is Mount Elbert. Mount Elbert is around 14,440 feet (4,401 m) high.

The Rockies are mostly fold mountains. Between 65 and 10 **million** years ago, the North American Plate pushed up against the Pacific Plate, forming high peaks.

The southern Rockies are where the highest peaks in the range are found. They go through Colorado, New Mexico, and southern Wyoming.

Life in the Rockies can be hard for people and animals. The winter is often long and cold, and snow covers the ground for a long time. The snow makes it hard for animals to find food there. However, animals like bears, mountain goats, bighorn sheep, and moose eat small plants that grow well in cold weather.

There are not many cities in the Rockies. This is because few people live in the mountains. It is hard for people to travel during the winter. However, there are people who come to the Rockies just to visit.

These mountain goats are standing on Mount Evans, in Colorado. Mountain goats can easily stay safe on rocky cliffs like this one.

There are many things people enjoy doing in the mountains. In the winter, snow skiing is a common sport. Mountains are good places to hunt and fish as well. Some people like to take pictures of mountain wildlife and the scenery. Brave people even like to climb to the tops of mountains!

Maybe you will climb a mountain one day, too. Perhaps you will go with your family or your class at school. A mountain is a good place to learn about Earth and wildlife. If you visit a mountain, you are on one of Earth's most interesting landforms.

Glossary

apart (uh-PAHRT) Into parts or pieces.

eroded (ih-ROHD-ed) Was worn away over time.

jagged (JAG-ed) Sharp and uneven.

layers (LAY-erz) Thicknesses of something.

llamas (LAH-muz) South American animals that look like camels but do not have humps.

magma (MAG-muh) Hot, melted rock inside Earth.

million (MIL-yun) A thousand thousands.

peak (PEEK) The very top of something.

protect (pruh-TEKT) To keep safe.

slope (SLOHP) A hill.

wrinkle (RING-kul) To fold or gather.

yaks (YAKS) Large oxen found in Central Asia.

Index

A
animals, 16, 20

C
crust, 8, 10, 12, 14

E
Earth, 6, 8, 12, 22

F
folding, 8
fold mountains, 8, 12, 18

L
layers, 8
llamas, 16

M
magma, 12, 14

N
North American Plate, 18

P
peak(s), 4, 8, 16, 18

plate(s), 8, 10, 18

R
range(s), 4, 18
rock(s), 8, 10, 12

S
slope, 10

Y
yaks, 16

Web Sites

Due to the changing nature of Internet links, PowerKids Press has developed an online list of Web sites related to the subject of this book. This site is updated regularly. Please use this link to access the list:
www.powerkidslinks.com/gzone/mountain/